Elizabeth Morgan

New York

Published in 2013 by The Rosen Publishing Group, Inc.
29 East 21st Street, New York, NY 10010

Copyright © 2013 by The Rosen Publishing Group, Inc.

All rights reserved. No part of this book may be reproduced in any form without permission in writing from the publisher, except by a reviewer.

Book Design: Michael Harmon

Photo Credits: Cover Brian Weed/Shutterstock.com; p. 5 Marie C Fields/Shutterstock.com; p. 7 Voronin76/Shutterstock.com; p. 9 Ryan McVay/Photodisc/Getty Images; p. 11 SunnyS/Shutterstock.com; p. 13 Ron Hilton/Shutterstock.com; p. 15 duckeesue/Shutterstock.com.

ISBN: 978-1-4488-8893-1
6-pack ISBN: 978-1-4488-8894-8

Manufactured in the United States of America

CPSIA Compliance Information: Batch #WS12RC: For further information contact Rosen Publishing, New York, New York at 1-800-237-9932.

Word Count: 18

# Contents

**My Shopping Trip**     4

**Words to Know**     16

**Index**     16

I see pie.

I see oranges.

I see juice.

I see eggs.

I see milk.

I see candy.

# Words to Know

candy

eggs

juice

milk

# Index

candy, 14
eggs, 10
juice, 8

milk, 12
oranges, 6
pie, 4